US
AND
THEM

US
AND
THEM

RAMIN GILLETT

YOKE *and* ABUNDANCE PRESS

US AND THEM

ISBN   979-8-88926-631-0   *Paperback*
         979-8-88926-632-7   *Ebook*

For the family we are struggling to become.

Contents

"The men where you live," said the little prince, *"raise five thousand roses in the same garden—and they do not find in it what they are looking for."*

Author's Note

In my dreams, I'm still a child running down a dusty road by a river near the house I grew up in. My feet hit the soft warm earth, and a cloud of dust trails behind me for as far as my small legs carry me. Even though it's winter and the rains haven't come yet, I know the water spirit, *Mami Wata*, lurks in the shadows ready to steal me away. My parents are at home waiting for me, and all I want is to drown in their love.

Some lives seem distant, like a faraway galaxy you can never quite reach. Maybe this is why I write poetry.

I live in the Appalachian Mountains now, and just the other morning it started to snow again. I'm not as young as I used to be, and Cameroon feels like a lifetime away. There was a time we chased grasshoppers as the sun went down, and streetlights lit up the southern sky. We put the grasshoppers into bags, filled to the brim, and later fried them in iron bowls over glowing charcoals at some other person's house. Never my own.

One day, not unlike any other day, I learned I was someone else, but not in a bad way. Just different.

Children called me *sarra*. They would see me coming in
the distance, and call out, *"Na sarra! Na sarra!"* and more
children would start emerging from behind the trees and
houses along the roadside. Very soon, a large contingency
would form around me, and a few courageous ones would
reach out to touch my hair or run their fingers down the
sides of my arms. I was theirs to keep, and I usually gave
in to their curiosity for a short while before scaring them
away with any sudden movement.

I hadn't always seen myself as being white. In fact, it
took a few years to learn this. I remember coming home
one day after school and staring at myself in the mirror
of my parents' bathroom. I must have been around six
at the time. It was the middle of the dry season, and my
entire body was covered in dust. My mother entered the
room, perplexed as to why I was looking so intently at
myself. She asked if I was feeling okay. When I didn't
respond, she asked again, and, in a voice that failed to
conceal my great disappointment, I said, "They are right.
I am different."

I'm not sure how that moment changed the way I related
to the world around me, but I know it did. As a child, I
navigated multiple cultural realities with ease, not caring
so much whether I fit in; but as I grew older I wanted
that elusive sense of belonging. Many of my closest childhood friends were anomalies like me, children of Indian,

American, Persian, German, and multiracial descent, but, nonetheless, we were all Cameroonian to varying degrees—one foot in and one foot out. As my teenage years crept by, my identity became increasingly rooted in an awareness that I never truly belonged anywhere.

As a child, my parents and I would spend our summers in Baltimore with my grandparents, who were originally from Florida and North Carolina. In America, I was also an anomaly, but in a different, more subtle way. In America, children didn't notice me like they did back home, but when they heard me speak, they would ask where I was from. They asked if lions roamed the streets, and if people lived in trees. I'd tell them about the lions I'd seen at the Baltimore Zoo, and that from the top of my tree I could see for miles and miles, and all the faces were as black as mine.

The world doesn't always conform to what we want or imagine it to be, and within that dissonance lies the pain and possibility to let go of antiquated ideas.

If we all share this common Earth that we call home, then why is it that we are taught to love one piece of it more than another? Why do we accept that a certain group has greater value over another? Why is the world created more for some than it is for others?

These poems are a search for the universal, an exploration of disparate lives that intersect in ways we do not always notice, but can certainly feel. I wrote this book

for anyone seeking connection that transcends borders,
ethnicities, and nationalities. My stories are our stories,
and your stories my stories.

In my search for home,
I found that home
was everywhere.

But this, too,
is privilege.

Introduction

When people ask me why I write, I say it's a curse. It's not a medal you put up on the wall and pride yourself for knowing that you have found this thing you love so much, to which you're dedicating yourself.

It's a curse because it never lets you forget you need to be writing (and writing well!), so you end up spending your whole life running away from it. It's like that term paper you had to submit at the end of the semester but, in this case, no one is requiring you to turn it in. The ball is in your court. No one's there to hold your hand. It's just you.

I have this recurring dream—a nightmare really--that comes to me in quiet moments of solitude or in that state of half-wakefulness when the reality of the world hasn't quite set in yet. In this dream a tree is slowly dying. Its leaves, once lustrous and green, have now become a deep shade of brown, like a hollowed-out walnut shell. In the distance, a storm is brewing, and the wind is blowing across the land. The tree is losing its leaves one after the other until it has no more to give, and all that is left is the howling of the wind.

They say the human body stops growing at the age of twenty-five, which is when we start to die (in a physical sense). I've been dying for a long time. Birthdays come and go, and each year I tell myself that this is the year I am going to start writing, and not just write but throw myself into it. Yet each year I find myself in the same predicament—a perpetual cycle of desire, conflict, and guilt.

Maybe it is not death we fear the most but regret, that is, the life that is half-lived—to have known our lives had a purpose and yet we squandered our years away.

I wrote my first story when I was twelve. It was a skeleton of a story about a traveler who stumbled upon a town where he quickly realized no one could see him. It wasn't until much later, when I took a fiction writing course in college, I discovered that a story unravels itself the more you work at it and all good writing is really good rewriting. How much had I written that ended up buried in the graveyard of forgotten stories? At this point, too many to remember.

The professor's name was Craig Nova, who I later discovered was an established figure in the literary world and, more importantly (to me), was a great teacher. I had finally found someone with whom I could speak about writing. We explored how a story, particularly a short story, bleeds at the end, how any story isn't about what happened but about what *didn't* happen, how one must feel the loneliness of a character, the importance of detail, and the art of showing, not telling.

Writing, and art in general, is a spiritual practice, however one wishes to define it. I write because I want to explore the nethermost regions of the human experience. It's about exploring truth, even if it is in an imagined universe. When I think back to my first story about the traveler, I wonder what would have happened if I had made him to be someone with less than noble intentions, an unscrupulous sort of fellow. Maybe a thief? But, more interestingly, what would've happened if he was a kind person? Would his newfound invisibility have changed him, and how? What would it tell us about the influence of power on good people? Maybe there really aren't any good people. Maybe we are all capable of incredible goodness and cruelty.

But maybe the story was really about me, and all the ways I was seen and not seen. Throughout my childhood, I unintentionally drew attention to myself simply by being different, and this feeling never quite escaped me. On a sunny day not too long ago, I was sitting outside a coffee shop when I caught myself in an old, familiar predicament, as natural as the sun's impenetrable glare beating against the expansive windows that separated me from the patrons sitting inside. I could feel their eyes—the eyes of everyone I could not see—bearing down on me, scrutinizing my every move.

Writing is a curse, and I have been cursed with this unquenchable need. And yet, I resist what I want the most. I do not know where this curse came from. Maybe we are all born with an itch. Mine started when I was a child, but I never thought of myself as a writer. Who does at that age? But as I grew older, the idea began to sink in until it became a reality. And I became a writer.

Why We Love Poetry

There will come a time,
as sure as the last breath
you'll ever take,
when you'll wish
you had loved
just a little more,

touched a little gentler,
waited a little longer,
spoken a little kinder.

I am here
to remind you
of all the things
we ignored.

Neither Here nor There

I come from a small family.
Three plates,
three spoons,
three movie tickets,
except there were no movie theatres
where I grew up.

Cameroon
is a country in Africa.
I say Africa
so people can relate.

If I say Cameroon,
I have to start again,
with Africa.
(Start big, and then drill down.)

But you're white, their eyes are screaming,
so I must clarify.

My dad is from Baltimore.
My mother is Iranian.

How did they end up in Cameroon?

How does one end up anywhere?
Why are you here?

If only I grew up in Alabama.

They call us third-culture children,
belonging nowhere and everywhere.
Half-in and half-out,
don't ask us where we belong.

There's this crazy idea that
you are me and I am you,
and without you, I would not exist.

I am still learning this.

My mother calls me *joonam*,
a term of endearment,
my dear, in Persian.

I am *mzungu* in Tanzania,
and in Catholic school
a teacher informed me I must be Lebanese,
but to everyone I was American.

I am simply my father's son.

I was born in Cameroon,
but in America I can be anything,

because I am white.

But what does that mean,
to be white,
other than being able to claim whatever you claim?
Italian, Greek, French, Slovak, Jewish.

I decided to be a white person for Halloween,
and isn't that as absurd
as it would
to be a Cherokee?

To be one thing can be quite boring,
but I wish I could relate to that,
to know I am this, and
you are that.

I am my father's son,
my mother's eyebrow;
and when my father's country
invades my mother's,
whose life shall I mourn?
Mine,
or yours?

Elephant Grass

In the evening, the lonely tractors near our house
smell cold, and remind me of money
that goes *clink clink clink,*
and that place daddy takes the car
on quiet sunny mornings.

I climb onto the broken leather seat.
The wheel is as big as a mountain
you can pinch from far away.

Up. Down. Left. Right.

The stick does not listen, but the round ball
feels smooth
like mommy's dress.

Up. Down. Left. Right.

Don't let me run you over.

The grass in the distance is so tall
they call it elephant. Elephant grass.

"Don't walk in elephant grass at night!
Snakes will find you!"

I am afraid of snakes, and so are chickens,
but I saw a chicken die once.

Daddy took a knife to its throat and sliced it sideways.
It melted like butter.

One morning, on my way to school,
I saw what a rock did to a man's head.
He was naked on the side of the road
with his arms stretched out like Jesus.
No one cried the way mommy cries sometimes,
but she doesn't know I see her through my fingers.

Fireflies fill the air like mist.
Their tiny bellies flicker in the cool air,
and I know it's time to go home.

Mangoes

black sticky fingers,
different than mine,
running through my
almost blond,
not curly hair,
reminding them of wet feathers.

followed by innocent laughter.

sitting on the front porch
with my mother
one lazy afternoon,
I ask,
Why am I white?

A Girl Called Light

I was nine when I lost my friend.
She was just a few years behind me,
sweeter than any of us
on her worst day.

Sometimes, when I try,
I remember her jet-black hair
against her light skin,
and how her eyes were
the essence of brilliance itself.

I remember, too, there was something
unreachable about her
that made us all want to be better,
more human.

Time has allowed me to stray and wander,
but I still find myself,
sifting through dust and clay
for that brief gift she put
into our small delicate hands—
that vision of what it means
to be human, to be better
than any of us ever were.

First Subway Ride

Women in tight dresses;
bubble gum, tattoos,
and nose piercings.

The lingering smell of cigarettes,
like the ones we passed around
at the school playground,
pretending to be older than we were.

Austere students in green and white uniforms,
no different than the one I wore
in the subcontinent.

Some things never change.

The doors open,
and they come marching in.

Tall deflated men,
men in suits,
suits that carried them
great distances,
distances I do not know.

The doors close,
and the air thins out.

Bodies rigid and unnatural,
skin touching skin,
ignoring the simple truth,
that we are all trapped in here, together.

Where Have You Been?

I met you in 2004
on an old nineties' television set.

I was twenty-two,
a college dropout.

You were me,
but I could hardly recognize you.

The years had passed, and I'd forgotten
so much about your life, but
most of all, I'd forgotten about you,
the person you were,
the person you are.

I forgot how confident
you were, and
how little you knew
of fear.

I forgot you stayed up late many nights
with that Walkman radio dad bought you
(on your summer trip to America),
scanning the AM airwaves
for some kind of greater truth.

Maybe we all forget what's most familiar,

because what's most familiar
is the air we breathe,
which, like our own scent,
is only odorless to us.

Watching you was like watching
someone I should know
stumbling through life,
oblivious of how beautiful
he truly is.

Hayti, 2016

Under the pale half-moon,
the banana fronds beat
to the rhythm of the soft
Caribbean breeze,
reminding me of the winter I left behind.

I am a stranger in a land
that smells like home,
galaxies away.

Ash and scorched earth,
mother, father,
Iwa.
You are here with me.

The young man with the potbelly
and Lakers jersey
roasting fish on a corrugated charcoal grill
speaks to me in Creole.

His name is Jean,
and I haven't told him
I leave the following morning.

He offers me a drink,
a grapefruit soda
he grabs from the fridge
and puts in my hand.

It's warm
like a heartbeat.

"No electricity again?"
"*Wi*," he answers
as he walks away.

He brings over the blackened cod,
toasted cassava, a bowl of *pikliz*,
and an ancient stew poured over a banana leaf,
passed down from the same hands

who filled me with life.
I am born again.

The bill is a piece of notepaper
with an old water stain and nebulous numbers
scribbled in red ink.

But when Jean finds out
it's my last night,
he's almost offended.

I can't pay for my meal.
He won't allow it.

"Non, non et non!"

Later he tells me in perfect English,
"You know, I love your country,
but ICE put me on a plane
and sent me back home."

The Return

One Florida afternoon,
late in the summer,

I got lost in a forest
of live oaks
and windy marshlands.

By a murky green pond
I spoke words ethereal and fluid of heart,
words I'd memorized long ago.

A gust of wind descended,
and everything danced and played.

I knew then how every leaf felt,
how every withered branch
stirred into existence.

I swallowed up the earthy musk,
and returned to a different beginning.

Warm Winters

After Brazil
I spent ten years
in Florida's swampland
of live oaks, aimless rivers,
and sleeping alligators.

It was the thickness
of the suffocating summer air that
finally drove me away,
and not
its interesting and schizophrenic politics,
which, like some kind of medieval sorcery,
made crusaders of secessionists.

But this is the South.

I was built rather for Miami
and its cultural ambiguity,
for the Puerto Ricans, Mexicans,
Nicaraguans, and Haitians,
for the three generations of Cuban
exiles, migrants, and refugees,
for the *los balseros*,
all chanting *viva Cuba libre*,
but who love America,
and dream of home
only ninety miles away.

For all of Florida's urban sprawl,
ever-shrinking everglades,
and rising waters,

I instead found respite in the solitude
of the Appalachian Mountains,
my ancestral homeland, also
the land of *Deliverance*,
as my folks in the North like to call it.

On an unusually warm day in December,
I met a lanky woman holding a Chihuahua
outside a Mediterranean eatery
in West Asheville.

She'd recently moved from Texas.

"In Texas everyone is welcome.
Here, I don't know.
They took down the statues.
They want to defund the police.
There's no place for me here."

I'm reminded of my grandfather's grandfather
who, during the outbreak of the Civil War,
volunteered to fight under the Confederate general
Edmund Kirby Smith,
nicknamed the Seminole (at West Point),

a botanist and regular supporter of the Smithsonian,
who, after a glorious defeat,
fled to Cuba to avoid the charge of treason.

His portrait now hangs
in one of the hallways at Vanderbilt,
where my grandfather spent his freshman year,

and I wonder,
if that was nostalgic.

Maybe we're all—
to lesser or greater degrees—
exiles, migrants, *los balseros*,
pawns of a history we did not write.

But the question remains,
like the rising tide along Florida's coastline,
are these United States as much for you
as they are for me?

A Pandemic Story

In the middle of the night
I hear the faint echo of my neighbor,
the young traveling nurse with the dog,
coughing from behind the wall.

There is silence before it rises again,
this time, like a distant avalanche.

I send her a text.
"Are you okay?"

She doesn't respond.

The next morning
she coughs all the way to her car
with her dog in tow
and drives away.

Later, she returns with a pharmacy bag
and a mask over her mouth.

She stays in the car,
her face buried in her hands.

The little white dog can't stop barking.

In the evening,
as the sun burns itself into oblivion,

I send her another message,
but she never responds.

I want to tell her:

There are people in this world
who wouldn't understand
our loneliness.

Time

How many friends I have lost
in those pacific waters of my mind,
where memories and moments intertwine
a thousand miles below.

I, under the bright red horizon,
can see for miles
as I scan for life,
a thousand miles below.

The Gift of Loneliness

I have entered the mid years of my life,
and I find myself asking the same questions
my mother asks
Why are you alone?
Why don't you have children?

I loved once,
for the better part of ten years—
a quarter of my life—
but I am relieved now
with lingering questions, like

How do you know you loved?

There was always something,
and other intangibles—

the tightness of my chest

a warm breeze in December

the smell of cherries
on her breath

the closing of a door.

I can't say I never thought about it,
but I am still learning
the gift of loneliness.

"You must become a father,"
my aunt says to me one wintry day in the kitchen.

But, what of loneliness? What of freedom?

"Loneliness is the price of freedom,
and you have too much love
to keep it all to yourself."

The spaces between are overcast
with shadows marking the inches of time,
the slowness of every breath.

An incoming storm,
an uncertain tide.

Why are you here?

The world around drifts
like unencumbered boats,
rubbing against each other,
bells clanking in the wind.

And then you hear it.
The ding of the phone.

The clouds disappear,
and it's sunny again.

"How are you?" she says.

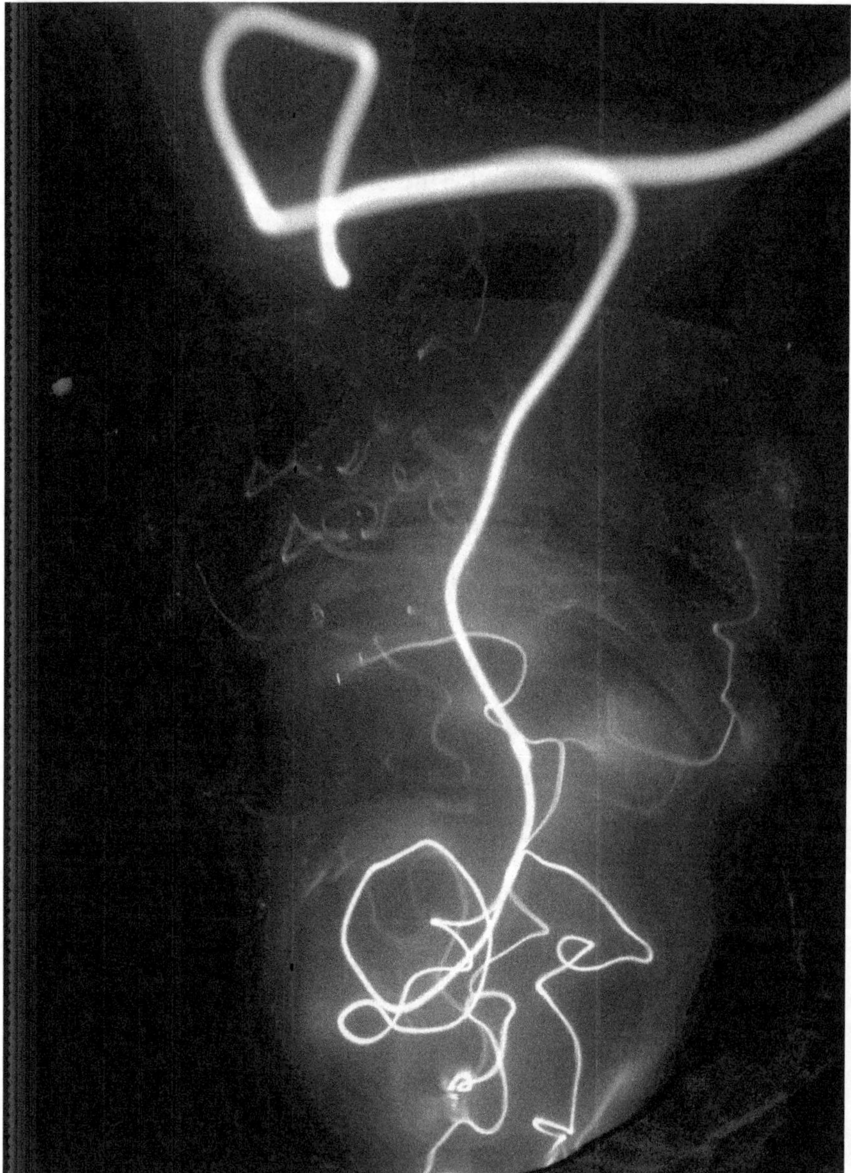

Death Is the Loneliest Journey

On the edge of a bed
in some tropical cosmos,
my body shakes in feverish delirium.

Quinine courses through my veins,
its bitter aftertaste
lingers in my mouth.

My body floats above me,
and when I reach for it,
I am my mother's child again,
and God is listening.

Please, listen.

I bring myself back
into whatever vessel this is.

The Law of Pain

Pain is like the water cycle,
or the law of thermodynamics.

Never created or destroyed,
but always transformed.

Series

In the first picture,
I am three, maybe four.

It's the year before we moved,
the reference point of all time,
on the banks of some river,
smothered between my parents.

And my sister, six years older,
with memories I do not have,
retreats into the background.

Where is she going?

The river is my prehistory,
the what of my life I do not know,
the place my parents fell in love,
a hole I will never fill.

In the second picture,
we are together,
just me and my parents,
for another goodbye,
in front of dormitory X
in state X.

Time has allowed me
to calculate sadness,
the loss in my mother's eyes,

for the second time.

But some things can be retrieved,
while others take much longer.

An eternity perhaps.
So isn't it wonderful
I have an eternity to find you?

The third picture hasn't happened yet,
and maybe it will be
the gleam in your eye
that I see again.

The Immigrant Story

We lost a house,
some farms,
a country,
my grandmothers' fattoush,
to come here

to be free,

and now I fear
I don't know who
my children are anymore.

Obscurement of Pain

I see it all the time;

parents surrendering their own existence
for their children's,
as though there were no more mountains to cross,
no other hope to live for,
but the hope in their child's eyes.

Theirs will be a bitter ending.

unfinished business

I fear I paid too little
for the wrinkles on my forehead

and that one day,
I'll be that guy
at the party
who won't know when
to stop talking
about you.

I fear this is a poem
about you,

that we will never
speak again
and I will
find you one day
happy,
and you won't see me.

I fear you knew
something of love
I am only learning
now.

I fear you will
never understand
what I did

and I will never find
the child you once were.

I fear I did not discover
all your regrets

and I never went to
my darkest places
to find you.

I fear you're a reflection of me.
And I am you, sometimes.

No. 79

I, the undersigned, Prisoner of War, belonging to the Army of the Trans-Mississippi Department, having been surrendered by General E. Kirby Smith, C. S. A., Commanding said Department, to Major General E. R. S. Canby, U. S. A., Commanding Army and Division of West Mississippi, do hereby give my solemn PAROLE OF HONOR, that I will not hereafter serve in the Armies of the Confederate States, or in any military capacity whatever, against the United States of America, or render aid to the enemies of the latter, until properly exchanged in such manner as shall be mutually approved by the respective authorities.

Residence _______________________

Done at _______________________

Approved:

The above named officer will not be disturbed by the United States Authorities, as long as he observes his parole, and the laws in force where he resides.

GEO. L ANDREWS,
Brig. Gen. U. S. A. and Provost Marshal General

GOVERNMENT PRACTISING SCHOOL
G.P.S.
BAMENDA

Laws of Nature

The moon follows the earth,
as the earth follows the sun.

Life is always just slightly out of reach,
and to this we owe our very existence.

Our feet, small and delicate,
learn to walk upon this ground.

Attraction begets attraction.

One day, when we discover
the wisdom of the sun,
we'll watch it grow dim,
discharging to each and every one of us
its last remnant of love.

And maybe by then,
we would have learned
to breathe together
in one last single breath.

Lies

I am a slave aboard this ship
moving with ferocity and stubborn agility
toward some magnificent tragedy.

Propelled by stories we're told
of valiant men and tragic heroes
who give their lives each day
for the service of a few
and the tears of many more.

A face among millions. A face long forgotten.

A thousand times I jumped
into those treacherous waters.
A thousand times I was dragged back
kicking and screaming,
my lungs filled with water,
spilling songs of places
I have long forgotten.

Rates of Exchange

The heart of a blue whale weighs 400 pounds,
or 181 kilos.

That is: one million dollars
stacked in five-dollar bills;
one Kawasaki Ninja 650;
300 squirrels;
680 Florida navel oranges;
754 Big Macs;
363,200 monarch butterflies;
61 AR-15s;

one million plastic nurdles
floating in the Atlantic Ocean.

The heart of a blue whale weighs
the last chapter of a book,
the hollowness of victory,
the unbearable silence of the ocean.

The Bankruptcy of Feeling

Another unarmed man is dead,
another neighborhood gone.

I must be sad, I say to myself.
But no longer are there feelings.

Only the idea of feelings.

I buy my feelings from those who have them,
from the newscasters,
politicians,
and judges.

And, just the other day,
in front of Starbucks,
I gave a dollar to a homeless man
with a noose around his neck.

We consume nature
the way we consume

      sex,

    school shootings,

      the happy meal,

entire countries,

        our collective trauma.

We consume nature
the way we consume

      our selves.

How It Will End

You can protest
your revulsion
to the mask.

After all,
it is the air
we commonly share
that you say
you cannot breathe,

in there.

It is your right, too,
that I breathe
your breath into me.

But there are other things
to consider,
like the white rhino,
the hawksbill sea turtle,
the bonobo,

who will soon stop breathing
altogether.

What about the fires,
the mystery gas,
the hatred, all made

for mass consumption,
courtesy of you and me?

What shall you breathe after
the other half
of the earth's lungs
are converted
into coffee tables?

Where They Went

Do you know that moment,
midsentence,
when
their eyes
have finally
lost their light,

and now

glaze over you
like a
cold mist
pouring over
a slab of glass?

An-other

In my culture
we never turn someone down.

In my culture
we are friends until you prove otherwise.

In my culture
we stop by unannounced.

In my culture
we bring each other food for no reason.

In my culture
we are not our pain.

In my culture
we cry together.

In my culture
we die together.

In my culture
we have a name for you.

In my culture
you are an exception to the rule.

In my culture
you are not us.

Schrödinger

How can light be
particle and wave,
and yet
you judge me
so simply?

Am I the
thinnest line
you've ever drawn
between you
and what you
do not understand?

In your eyes
I behold the wonder
of my own existence.

A Paralysis

I feel like I never
have enough time

time to read the onslaught
of *National Geographic*
and *New Yorker* magazines,
stockpiling into the Tower of Pisa
in my upstairs hallway

time to plan for how
much food I'll need to grow
in my shoebox backyard
when the apocalypse comes,
and if the neighbors will turn
on each other

time to get to know my neighbors,
particularly the young Afghan couple
who recently moved into the house
across the street

time to plan where we'll
be sourcing our drinking water
in the year 2030

time to call my friends,
even the ones who won't answer,
and tell them
they are sorely missed

time to maintain at least
one coherent thought
in my head, before being
stymied by an assault
of ads and memes

time to figure out
the answer to the equation of
how many additional catastrophes
we will need to endure
over X period of time

before we finally realize that
the way we held each other
for those two weeks
in September of 2001
will, one day,
encompass
the
entire
world.

$20.64

The end of the day is near,
and I'm flipping through the channels,
searching the airwaves
for some semblance of truth.

Above the talking heads of the men in charge,
beyond the voices who know it all,
through the barrage of noise,
I finally find what I'm looking for.

My soothsayer.
My truth teller.

It's written all over her face,
tears as real as cicadas
screeching outside my window.

I try to say something,
but the cacophony of men
drowns me out.

Are you there? she asks.

Yes I am! I shout back.

Why are you crying? I ask.

She says something, but I can barely hear her.
She is holding a piece of paper, something official.
She points to it and starts screaming again.

What is it? I ask but she can't hear me.

She closes her eyes as though to compose herself.
She starts shouting again,
and, this time,
all the talking stops.

I lost my daughter today, she says.

The piece of paper—$20.64.
Her daughter's last paycheck.

phil-an-thrope

(Not to be confused with mis-an-thrope)

200 dollars for a plate
of roast duck and fingerling potatoes
gives you a taste of America.

20 cents to a nine-year-old Syrian boy
in a refugee camp in Turkey
gives you a sense of purpose.

While you hardly touch your food,
he has enough bread and beans
to last him three days.

A Clarification

I was once accused
of being a socialist,
so I took the man's
calculated hand
that still believed
in fairy tales,
like
trickle-down economics,
and put it on my heaving chest

and I asked him,
"Do you feel that?

That is the opposite of capitalism."

Veins Like Lace

What is death to an albatross, a sea urchin,
a gazelle, an orca, a saola?

What about a white rhinoceros,
or the golden-eyed lacewing
that flew in through my front door late last night.

I tried to shoo you away
but you were stubborn,
like many of us are.

And then I lost you,
even though I searched the stairs
and the rugs that went
all the way to dad's Steinway
we were never allowed to touch.

Now, the next morning,
you lie lifeless on the cold granite countertop
in the kitchen of my childhood.

I touch your fleshy abdomen to see if you are alive,
but you are quiet as a feather.

Was yours a slow and painful death, I ask.

Your wings are translucent green
with bright veins like lace,
twice the length of your slender body.

Scientists call you Chrysopa oculata.

But to be honest, I didn't know what you were
till I took your picture
and searched for you on my phone.

You are born from silk cocoons
attached to the underside of leaves.
You like to eat nectar, pollen,
and honeydew.

You are
a nocturnal assassin,
ruthless with mites
and aphids—

any gardener's best friend.

Oh, how I wish, dear lacewing,
to have known
so easily my own purpose,
which yours
inevitably brought you
to me.

cosmic

we designed the world
as though it
was created in six days,

as though there were ten trillion trees,
ten trillion rivers,
ten trillion reefs,
ten trillion white rhinos.

ten.

not two.
not three.
not six.

ten.

we designed the world for ourselves.

now, I must think of
your children
and your grandchildren
who will one day find the cheetah,
and the mountain gorilla,
sitting on a museum shelf
next to the dodo,
and they will ask you,

what happened?

Veneer

Sometimes at dusk, or
late in the afternoon
when the dust has finally settled,
I find myself driving through
an old neighborhood
of freshly restored row houses and
resettled gardenias,
cautious of any unintended run-ins
with my own childhood.

But these streets and enclosures,
like perfectly sculpted icicles,
have become empty
of laughter and madness.

The houses are shells
of stolen memories,

and the dark ridges along the oak floors
in the upstairs corner bedroom
where something heavy once fell,
remind you that, even
before the pioneers,

on these lonely streets,
we too once existed.

Bad Lands

The air outside is as dry as the land
around the gas station.

A scorching breeze sends tumbleweeds down the two-
lane road,
and dust clouds rise like a tide
casting a looming shadow across the land.

Alone without traveler or companion,
the road is no better off than the charred earth.

Hollowed-out cars flank its sides,
and cracks, like tributaries, have shattered the asphalt,
creating spider webs for as far as the eye can see.

The earth is forcing its way through.

Inside, a transistor radio
plays an old tune,
and later, an old familiar voice scratches through
the weathered and fragile speakers.

"Well, there you have it folks.
That was the Jackson 5,
who just announced their departure
from Motown Records after learning
they were earning just 2.8 percent of royalties.
You heard that right folks—2.8 percent.
Now back to the weather, Bill."

"Thanks Bob. It looks like rain
will continue into the evening,
but a nice push of drier air
will clear the skies up by morning.
Expect temperatures to drop by..."

The radio stops.

A passing gale sucks the door open
and a cloud of dust drifts through the entryway,
glazing the floors;
discarded newspapers,
empty shelves,
and, all the way in the back,
a faded Confederate flag,
still hanging on three loose nails.

Below it,
inscribed in blood, are the words,
In God We Trust.

A Little Background

One morning, many years ago,
sixty-three migrants showed up at my door.

They wanted me to feed them,
clothe and shelter them.

But I had a small house,
not even a full bedroom,
and hot water
just enough for
a single bath,
and all my harvest
I sold at the market.

When the leader of the pack approached,
I shook my head
and smiled…for effect.

When they were on their way,
a child shouted, "N——!"
and farther down the road,
another cried out, *"Abd!"*
and farther down, "Squaw!"
"Spic!"
"Kaffir!"

Many years later, when our fields had turned brown,
they came back, but this time
they brought carriages of gold, wheat,

and cattle of every color
and size.

They moved with the drum, and
in long bright robes,
brought gifts for every house,
delivered in large porcelain bowls.

We looked to the bowls,
with eyes of disdain,
and bided our time
until such a mockery
we could stand
no longer,

and one day,
on a particularly sunny afternoon,
we went for the pitchforks,
hammers, ropes, and guns,
and like that,

we took care of them.

On War

Beware, beware of the conquerors.
But also of the conquered,
and the blood that still stains our streets.

Do you remember Germany
after World War I,
Russia
after the Cold War,
the South
after the Civil War?

Some arguments never die,
but are reborn and recast
with new actors
playing the same part,
using the same old script.

I don't want your outworn ideas;
tell me something new.

Tell me you feel my child's heartbeat,
as he lies here dying
because you loved the play
more than beauty itself.

Tell me you made
the tanks, and the bombs
knowing that this day would finally come,

that we would pay the price
for the war inside you.

Show me a new play.
Give me a different ending.

Phantasmagoria

A friend of a friend you met at a pool party
spends her days on a yacht off the coast of Italy.

Your roommate from college
test-drives Lamborghinis in Denver,
says his life is a vacation.

You scroll past the world
through the lens in your hands.

Digital prototypes of yourself
become an aspiration.

The homeless boy you ran into at Hagia Sophia
just got engaged.

Your best friend from thirty years ago.
Single now.
A dad you might never become.

The affable waiter in San Juan
who served you the $60 lukewarm Wagyu steak
is an illegal immigrant.
Parents killed in Guatemala.

An acquaintance who skis the Swiss Alps every January
owns his own island.
Career unknown.

Chantelle from back home. Chantelle you kissed.
Chantelle you promised tomorrow to.
Chantelle who took the morning-after pill.
Chantelle the cashier.
Chantelle struggles to pay rent.

Your neighbor next door,
who collects your mail whenever you travel,
is slowly dying of cancer.

In Celebration
of
Small Things

I wanted success,
not knowing that
success exists

in the spaces
between breaths
and bruises

between surrenders,
anniversaries,
and I-love-yous

between those we have hurt
and the awakening of our souls

between who we have become
and our return to
the innocence of childhood

between the world that is
and what
it could be

between you
and
me

between us

and

them.

Child of the Earth

It was late in the night,
when you ran to me
and pressed yourself in my arms.

The wind outside was howling,
and the water was rising again.

In the distance,
across the flooded fields,
a solitary light flickered.

How small you were,
curled up against me.
You were no longer the little girl
I was holding on to.

I wanted to protect you
from all of it,
but my first duty
was to make you
stronger,
stronger than the world
could
ever destroy.

"What is it?" I asked,
though I didn't have to.

Your eyes were someplace else,
on some distant ephemeral world
you could barely grasp.

This was just the beginning, I thought to myself.

The world was changing
and so were you.

For Whom Do You Cry?

Just last year, at the dinner table,
there were four place settings,
and now there are three.

They say we are a divided country,
and on this, we agree.
But we are mothers,
romantics, idealists, cynics,
drifters—
visionaries.

We wear our pain on our chest,
decorations of some war we fought,
or didn't fight but instead inherited,
emblems of everything we despise in each other.

We brought our pain from the old world
and, on this land, we built a spectacular edifice
and called it ours, and our children's,
but only ours.

This land is my land,
this land is your land.

Our memory ends with us,

"But I am here too," she says.
"Tell me your pain,
and I will show you my scars

that make you fear me so.
Or is it you that you fear?

And will you listen,
as you would to your child,
your lover,
your friend?

Am I still the conquered
as I stand here asking,
For whom do you cry?"

Glass Houses

We live along tributaries
and escarpments,
marshlands and cityscapes,
forests and landfills,
broken bridges and suburbia,
along twisted highways
and roads going everywhere
and nowhere, intertwined,
majestic and full of misery.

On dreams we build our castles,
atop ancient and forgotten civilizations,
locking ourselves away from within,
only to want more than we've found.

Along back roads and forgotten highways
lie the austere prisons of our imaginations,
languishing in decay.

Our houses are growing old,
and we have outgrown them.

For the Missing Boy

The world changed on a Thursday
when my shift ended,
but the truth is
it had been changing all along.

We walked a long way,
through crumbling underpasses,
over thinning prairies and mountaintops,
silent and dry
as the wind blowing across
these scorched lands.

How green it must have looked
to the pilgrims when they first arrived.

They took you away from me,
not because they wanted to,
but because of their own indifference.

Your last words were,
I love you.
I love you.
I love you.
I love you.
I love you.

We are America's leftovers.

For Mahsa

You are not the lamp.
You are the light within the lamp.

The lamp can be broken,
but you,
my dear,

will
never
be
extinguished.

Principles of Change

You are the world.

You are what is
in front of you,
above and below you.

You are the cabdriver from the East Side
who looks at you like you're nobody,

the homeless woman on 2nd
whose entire life fits into a grocery cart,

the city official waving goodbye
as the garage door closes on her,

the tree next to the house you grew up in,
the tree you climbed and conquered,
the tree that was born before your daddy,
the tree I'm looking at right now.

You asked me what I smoked
so I asked,
What did YOU smoke?
What tales did you hear?

Who told you
you're the house you bought,
the clothes you wear,
the color of your hair,

the car you drive,
the job that could've gone to any
one of 239 people?

Who are you when the world
thinks you're ugly,
unnecessary,
disposable?

Who are you when you look
into the mirror one day and
do not recognize yourself?

Who are you when all this vanishes
and slips out of your fingers like fog?

"Are you the world then? Am I ugliness too?" you ask.

"Yes," I say.
"You are all of it,
and so you must
change you."

Will You Do This?

For too long,
we've hidden behind
our words,
our humor,
our pain.

I can't see you,
because I can't see
myself in you.

I can't see you,
because I can't see
my own pain.

My pain,
like my own veil,
is what you see
and what I cannot see,
because it's the very eye
through which I see you.

Let's meet then,
you and I.

Let's meet
on some
distant shoreline
under moonlight,
and slowly take off
our veils.

How to Love

What is love? the boy asked.

But to suffer, the old man said.

Its language is of loss and discovery, he continued.
But like the shadow that lives between light and dark,
it can only be understood as one.

Always one, he repeated.

What do we lose? the boy asked.

The old man waited a while.

Your old self, he finally said.

The journey of forgiveness begins
in the hearts of the ones we wronged.

Their release
is our release.

The journey to want to be forgiven
is also the journey to forgive.

Two Roads

Beyond the brambles,
beyond the regret,
beyond yourself
is a path of little-known consequence.

For the road less traveled is yours
and no one else's.

Don't you see it?
It is unknown and full of fear.

But also,
lightness unimagined.

Gratitudes

I am deeply humbled by everyone who believed in the possibility of this book and who powered its publication by making an early purchase. Zulma L. Ibanez, Virginia Lintz. Britt Patterson, Theresa Jones, Orlando Morondos, Takashi Mbako, Austin Wade Garcia, Antoinette Njombua-Fombad, Rita Priest, Sorangi De Leon, Seth Watts, Francisco Garcia, Ramona Covrig, Michelle Wagner, Katie Lopez, Elham Smith, Christina Farber, Megan Bass, Matheus Souza, Sahar Frooghi, Bahamin Behipour, Joseph Mazzaferro, Valeria Herzer, David Puwol, Daniel Stettner, Rebecca Clifford, Scotts Higeoka, David Gillette, Lisa M. Haynes, Dana Morgan Gillett, Amy Quinn, Donald R. Davis, Amanda Gross, Bejan Bahai, Lisa Kinsell, Amani McHugh, Heather Donihe, Marianne Sprangers, Eric Koester, Tracey Hickox, Malika Ramrattan, Summer Moore, David B. Gillett, Oloro McHugh, Nahal Bushrui, Annie Cheek, Lawrence Kline, Rebecca J. Williams, Linda Khadem, Katharine Day, Renee Glinski, Cornelia "Amina" Rutledge, Mary Jane Volkmann, Gretchen Hill, Omid Akale, Stephen Ford, Melissa Howard, Brenda Puwol, Martha Bhaskaran, Elizabeth Mcguire-Robertson, David Pittman, Sanam Symboli, Sarah Kloewer, Manuel Peralta,

Elga Agbaw, Kim Kruse, Sam Toloui, Christian Smith, Ben Leiker, Jessica Guillen, Michelle Tannebaum, Colitta M. Bayung, Jennifer Lederman, Jessica Rohani, Claudia Maturell, Nabil Mansouri, Shaidu Kiven, Inee Hamidi, Jacqueline Odess-Gillett, Marshallyn Phillips, Brent Ferraro, Isar Mahanian, Chitra Badii, Maeve Pinto Math, Bart Shull, Todd Westover, Afshin Cohen, Alisha Wielfaert, Prashant Goel, Sara Kubik, Kathryn Henderson, Marlene McConnell, Jen Hampton, Shay Cooper, Monica Merenda, Sierra Moffett, Soha Modir, Viktoryia Claypool, Frances Worthington, Maryanne Edmundson, Kevin White.

If I was remiss in including your name, it was out of my own human frailty, and I hope you do let me know so we can correct it in future editions.